PINEHURST: GOLF, HISTORY, and the GOOD LIFE

• A U D R E Y   M O R I A R T Y •

SPORTS
MEDIA
GROUP

All inquiries should be addressed to:
Sports Media Group
An imprint of Ann Arbor Media Group LLC
2500 S. State Street
Ann Arbor, MI 48104

Printed and bound at Edwards Brothers, Ann Arbor, MI

09 08 07 06 05 1 2 3 4 5

Library of Congress Cataloging-in-Publication Data
Moriarty, Audrey, 1951-
  Pinehurst : golf, history, and the good life / Audrey Moriarty.
     p. cm.
  ISBN10: 1-58726-179-0 (alk. paper)
  ISBN13: 978-1-58726-179-4
  1. Golf--North Carolina--Pinehurst--History. 2. Pinehurst (N.C.)--History. I. Title.

GV983.P57M67 2005
796.352'09756'352--dc22

                                        2004027005

Jacket and book design by Somberg Design
www.sombergdesign.com

CONTENTS

INTRODUCTION

The Tufts Archives is a treasure trove of information on the history of the village of Pinehurst, North Carolina, as well as on turn-of-the-twentieth-century social customs, fashion, and lifestyle. Within the walls lies the complete history, document by document, of the growth of the village and the simultaneous growth of the sport of golf in this area. On display are items made by the Tufts Silver Plate Company, china that was used in 1895 at the Holly Inn, playing cards with bullet holes made in them by Annie Oakley, decorated holiday menus from the Carolina Hotel (the "Queen of the South"), hand-colored postcards, a Tufts soda fountain, hundreds of original drawings made by golf course architect Donald Ross, and many of the more than 100,000 photographic images that are owned by the archives.

These images are mainly the work of C. E. Vale, E. L. Merrow, E. C. Eddy, and John G. Hemmer. Vale began photographing Pinehurst in the summer of 1895, documenting construction work in the village and other contemporary scenes. Merrow began assisting Vale around 1900 and captured much of the early golf. Eddy did some of the first aerial photography (which had to have been harrowing) and also created beautiful panoramic images of the village. Hemmer worked as the official photographer of Pinehurst for forty years, and very little escaped his lens. Fortunately, the vast majority of his wonderful work is in the archives. The result is an unbroken pictorial history of the first several decades of the village.

In the early 1970s the Diamondhead Corporation purchased Pinehurst, Inc., from the descendants of James Walker Tufts, the founder of the village of Pinehurst. The Tufts Foundation was formed then and endowed the Tufts Archives. However, an endowment that was deemed adequate in the early 1970s is no longer sufficient to support the operations of a modern institution that faces serious preservation issues and requires special and costly climate controls to overcome them.

Due to the enormous amount of material housed in the Tufts Archives, this book makes no attempt to be complete. It provides, however, a representative sampling of the hundreds of images that tell the unique story of the village of Pinehurst. The publication of this book is an effort to support and preserve the Tufts Archives— not only for those who live and work in the Pinehurst area, but also for those who find themselves drawn to one of golf's most revered destinations. Proceeds from this book will go directly to the Tufts Archive.

Audrey Moriarty
Executive Director, Tufts Archives

Leonard Tufts was born in 1788 in Charlestown, Massachusetts. A blacksmith by trade, he married
Hepzibah Fosdick, three years his senior, in 1821.

Chapter 1

THE BEGINNINGS OF A VILLAGE

On February 11, 1835, a son was born to Leonard and Hepzibah Tufts of Charlestown, Massachusetts. They named him James Walker, and he grew to be an extraordinary man who eventually purchased a barren patch of land and turned it into one of America's foremost resort locations, Pinehurst, North Carolina.

Leonard Tufts died when James was sixteen. To help support his mother, the young man became an apprentice at Samuel Kidder & Company, a Charlestown apothecary. During his apprenticeship, he also sold lozenges, almanacs, and sweet fern cigars that he made himself. On the side, he experimented with making chewing gum. After completing a six-year apprenticeship, James opened his own apothecary in Somerville, Massachusetts, and worked long hours preparing remedies and extracts. Four years later he opened a second store in Medford, and he eventually purchased shops in Winchester, Woburn, and Boston, creating one of the earliest drugstore "chains."

During this time, James met and married Mary Emma Clough. The couple had four children, but only daughter Mary Gertrude and son Leonard survived childhood. James soon began manufacturing items for other apothecaries and, by age twenty-seven, created a complete line of soda fountain supplies and flavored extracts. He also developed his own soda fountain apparatus and started the Arctic Soda Fountain Company. Tufts' soda fountains were made of Italian marble, block tin, and heavy silver plate. He also manufactured functional silver-plated items such as napkin rings, toothpick holders, baskets, urns, jewelry boxes, and casters. All items were made out of quadruple silver plate and bore the Tufts mark and number.

In 1876 a Centennial Exhibition was held in Philadelphia to celebrate the birth of the Republic and the first 100 years of progress. On exhibit were numerous gadgets and inventions, including a slice of the cable used to secure the Brooklyn Bridge, the first typewriter, an early telephone, and a Corliss Steam Engine. Visitors could also watch newspapers being printed, logs being sawed, material being sewn, and wallpaper being made. In the midst of all this stood a thirty-foot-high Arctic Soda Fountain with elaborate spigots, hanging ferns, and a chandelier. It also sprayed perfume.

James W. Tufts and fellow businessman Charles Lippincott paid $50,000 for exclusive rights to sell soda water beverages and ice cream sodas during the exhibition. They also created an early instant beverage by selling packets of dried herbs that could be used to create root beer.

In 1877 James published a catalog that offered simple-to-fancy soda fountains ranging in price from a few hundred dollars to $2,500. Most of the fountains were elaborate, bearing multiple spigots, cherubs, figures of women, children or animals, plants, ferns, or towers. The catalog also offered mineral waters, siphons, beer attachments (for ginger and root beers—James was a teetotaler), and other items that he had invented or perfected, such as carbon dioxide gas generators for carbonation, tabletop fountains, bottling machines, and tumbler washers.

In 1891 Tufts merged with the Charles Lippincott Company of Philadelphia, A. D. Puffer & Sons of Boston, and the John Matthews Firm of New York to create the American Soda Fountain Company. James was named president of the new company. After four years, Tufts sold his portion of American Soda Fountain Company for $700,000. With no interest in retiring at the age of sixty, he came up with a plan to build a resort in the southeastern part of the United States.

At the time, many well-to-do residents of the northeast were in the habit of traveling to Florida to avoid the harsh New England winters. James was well aware of this annual flight, as well as the fact that many people all over the country suffered from consumption (later known as tuberculosis). Never a hearty man himself, Tufts hoped to find a restful and healthy area that the sickly could visit and where they could hopefully become cured. The first step, however, was to find a location. James had heard about the curative powers of the North Carolina Sandhills from an acquaintance in Boston, the Reverend Edward Everett Hale. Hale, chaplain of the U.S. Senate and author of *The Man Without a Country*, was a well-known reformer and humanitarian. With his assistance and inspiration, Tufts began planning his mid-south resort.

After visiting the Sandhills in 1895, James purchased some 600 acres (the area that is now the racetrack, the country club, and most of the Village Green) from Luis A. Page. He made several other purchases and eventually acquired about 6,000 acres for roughly $1.25 per acre. Many residents in the area believed the man from Massachusetts had been cheated, that the land wasn't worth "but eighty-five cents"

THE BEGINNINGS OF A VILLAGE **9**

per acre. This was because the land that Tufts had purchased was part of the Pine Barrens, an area that had been logged extensively, and was used by the turpentine, pitch, and tar industries. Trees selected by the turpentine industry were specially cut in "v-shaped" downward angles that allowed pinesap to flow into a flat surface that was cut into the tree. This section was referred to as "the box," and experienced workers could cut a box in ten minutes. As the years passed, however, additional slashes were cut (or an entire new box) that weakened the trees to the point that they simply fell over, blew over, or died. The remaining dried resins and sap formed a highly flammable residue that frequently resulted in intense flash fires. (One such conflagration threatened Tufts' dream in 1898. Fortunately, backfires were quickly set and a potential disaster was avoided.)

In spite of the damage that his new property had suffered from logging and fire, James Tufts was determined to create an attractive and welcoming village in the North Carolina Sandhills. Consequently, he called on the firm of Olmsted, Olmsted & Elliot. Frederick Law Olmsted had become famous for designing Central Park in New York City. It was Olmsted's belief that cities should be places of beauty and not just commerce centers. His plans included scenic and recreational areas, and he attempted to follow the curve of the land rather than the traditional use of right angles that resulted in the grid pattern that was common in cities of the day. He also believed in a landscaped "transitional" area between homes and public streets, and that buildings should fit naturally into their surroundings.

Following his discussions with Tufts, Olmsted agreed to develop a plan for a fee of $300. After Olmsted began showing early signs of dementia, it was decided that associate Warren Manning would be the one to make visits and supervise the work. Manning began visiting the site in 1895 and immediately took charge of planning the new foliage for the village. He acquired over 200,000 plants, with about 47,000 coming from France. Local plantings were also brought in from neighboring swamps, and many were cultivated and propagated on-site. The soil was poor and sandy, and grasses were difficult to grow. The planned village green became a pine grove. Eventually, Manning learned which plants thrived and grew successfully in the mid-south.

Tufts' original plan had been philanthropic. His intention was to not sell any land or make a profit, but to merely create a beautiful health resort where consumptives could recover with family and friends. Unfortunately, he was forced to change those plans when he learned that tuberculosis was highly contagious.

At the age of twenty-one, James started his own business in Somerville, Massachusetts. In just a few years, he created one of America's earliest pharmacy chains with stores in Medford, Winchester, Woburn, and Boston. At twenty-seven he had another business, the Tufts Soda Apparatus Company, manufacturing items for other apothecaries and featuring a complete line of flavored extracts and soda fountain supplies, some of which he invented himself. His business eventually became the Arctic Soda Fountain Company, offering by catalog an extensive line of soda fountains and functional silver plate items.

James' son Leonard, shown here circa 1876, inherited Pinehurst after his father died in 1902.

James married Mary Emma Clough on October 30, 1862, after a nearly four-year engagement. Mary and James had four children, but only two, Mary Gertrude (born June 11, 1868) and Leonard (born June 30, 1870), survived. James and Mary (his first cousin once removed) were devoted to each other and were married for thirty-nine years.

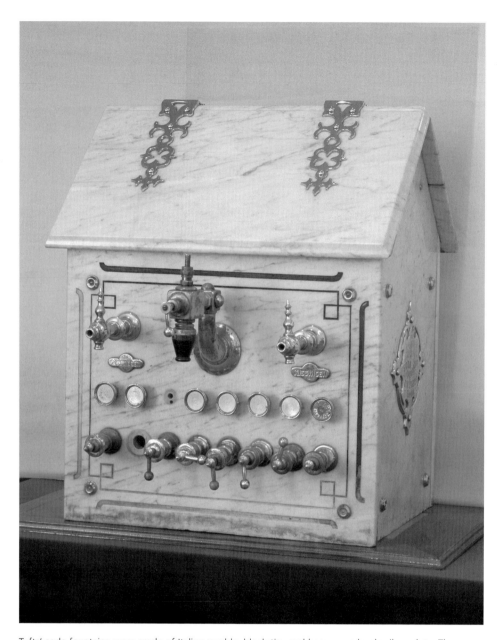

Tufts' soda fountains were made of Italian marble, block tin, and heavy quadruple silver plate. The Cottage model shown was a simple fountain for small businesses, but the Tufts fountains built for hotels and larger businesses were quite elaborate, often featuring multiple spigots, cherubs, figures of women or animals, tumbler washers, and attachments for root and ginger beer.

In 1876 a Centennial Exhibition was held in Philadelphia to commemorate the birth of the Republic. Among the many items on display was a thirty-foot-high Arctic soda fountain that featured elaborate spigots, hanging ferns, and a chandelier.

Tufts' idea of building a health resort led him to North Carolina. Northwest of the town of Southern Pines, he selected an area of land known locally as the "Pine Barrens." In July 1895 he purchased 600 acres from Luis A. Page for about $1.18 per acre. Some of the local residents felt Tufts had been cheated. The land was so rough and rugged that one man said it wasn't worth more than eighty-five cents an acre.

Tufts' sport of choice was roque, a version of croquet.

In the 1890s logging was a big industry in the Pine Barrens, and longleaf and loblolly pines were the most sought-after timbers. The logs were taken to the Cape Fear River and floated on rafts to the market in Wilmington, North Carolina. Throughout the Sandhills, the timber was actually more valuable than the land.

For years the Pine Barrens had been logged extensively and used for the turpentine, pitch, and tar industries.

GENERAL PLAN
FOR THE VILLAGE OF
PINEHURST
MOORE CO. N C
SCALES

100   0   100   200   300   400   500 Ft.

10 0   50   100   150 METERS

OLMSTED OLMSTED & ELIOT
LANDSCAPE ARCHITECTS, BROOKLINE, MASS.
WARREN H. MANNING, LANDSCAPE ARCHITECT IN CHARGE.

KEY SHOWING LOCATION OF PRINCIPAL BUILDINGS.

1. HOLLY INN.
2. CASINO.
3. VILLAGE HALL.
4. THE MAGNOLIA.
5. PINE GROVE HOUSE.
6. SCHOOL HOUSE.
7. GENERAL STORE AND OFFICES.
8. PINE REST.
9. THE CEDARS.
10. THE PALMETTO.
11. THE OAKS.
12. THE HANOVER.
13. THE BEACON.
14. THE TREMONT.
15. THE MARLBOROUGH.
16. THE DARTMOUTH.

TYPICAL SECTION OF ROAD

CROQUET AND TENNIS GROUNDS

PINE GROVE

⑱

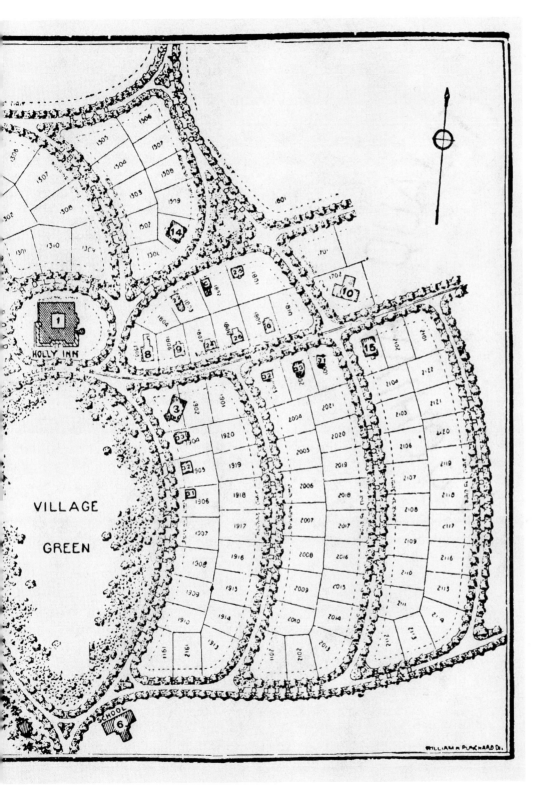

Tufts wanted his village to be as beautiful and appealing as possible, so he hired the New York firm of Olmsted, Olmsted & Elliot (developer of Central Park) to create a plan for the village.

Warren Manning was one of the ten original founders of the American Society of Landscape Architects. He was employed by Frederick Law Olmsted from 1888 to 1895 and worked on plans for the Biltmore Estate in Ashville, North Carolina, and park systems for Milwaukee, Minneapolis/St. Paul, Louisville, and Cincinnati. At Pinehurst, Manning oversaw all of the work.

While James was developing Pinehurst, his son, Leonard, had been active in the soda fountain business in Massachusetts. After his father died in 1902, Leonard discovered that inheriting his village would keep him busy in North Carolina. Leonard was very interested in the agriculture business of Pinehurst and became a talented animal breeder. He also brought agricultural conventions and meetings to the village and was given an award by the state for his work in agricultural development and in the building of better roads.

In 1904 Leonard moved to Pinehurst with his wife, Gertrude, whom he had married in June 1895. She and Leonard had four children: Richard, Esther, Albert, and James. Gertrude became very active in the Girl Scouts. In 1958, eighteen years after her death, the Central Carolina Girl Scout Council dedicated Camp Gertrude Tufts in her honor.

Richard's first wife, Alice Bogart Vail, was born on February 22, 1900. She was very athletic and a good horsewoman. Alice and Richard were also tournament-class tennis players. She died on December 20, 1961. In October of 1964, Richard married Vandy Cape Palmer. She was a singer and a music critic and she and Richard shared a love of music. Vandy passed away in March 1974, after nearly ten happy years of marriage.

When Leonard died in 1945, his son Richard S. Tufts became the president of
Pinehurst, Inc. He had attended Harvard University and MIT, served in the U.S.
Navy, and learned how to play golf from Donald Ross. It was Richard who brought
Pinehurst to worldwide prominence as a golf mecca, and his contributions to the
game of golf have been profound and lasting. He authored two books on golf,
The Scottish Invasion and *The Principles Behind the Rules of Golf*, and was
president of the USGA in 1956–1957. He died in 1980.

The Holly Inn, the first of the hotels in the village, is shown under construction. It was located at the head of the Village Green where the view across to the Pine Grove was originally unobstructed.

Chapter 2
EARLY DEVELOPMENT

As the plan for the village took shape, goods and supplies were shipped into the nearby town of Southern Pines and transported to the site. Construction workers and shippers began referring to the settlement as "Tuftstown" or "Pinalia." James Tufts heard people using those names while he was staying at the Ozone Hotel in Southern Pines. He disliked both and actually chose the name "Pinehurst" from a list of potential names for Martha's Vineyard published in a northeastern newspaper. James wrote to the person who had suggested Pinehurst, got permission to use it, and officially named the village.

Tufts wanted to create a village where people of all means could afford to visit. He knew their needs would be varied, so he decided to build an assortment of private cottages, rooming houses, and hotels. Additional necessities, from food to diversion, would also have to be provided.

Between July and December of 1895, an unbelievable amount of building was completed. By the end of the year, the Holly Inn, over thirty cottages, and a few rooming houses had been built. Most of the cottages and rooming houses—each named after a plant or location in New England—were wood-framed structures that offered one or more bedrooms. Few had kitchens. In an advertising brochure, the cottages were said to be "very attractive in appearance, and are tastefully and substantially built from plans of eminent Boston architects." At that point the Casino, the Pine Grove House, the Palmetto, water supply towers, a power supply building, a trolley line, and greenhouses were all in operation. Streets for the village were also being constructed and landscaped by Warren Manning. A department store, the Village Hall, and the Magnolia Inn would soon be built.

By 1899 the Holly Inn had been expanded, the 250-room Carolina Hotel had opened, and, by combining the Oaks and Hanover cottages, the Berkshire Hotel had

The Holly Inn opened on New Year's Eve in 1895 with twenty guests. This "modern" facility had electric lights, steam heat, a billiard room, a card room, a call bell in each room, and the finest hair mattresses.

been created. The village also had its own fire department and livery stable. Over the next few years, additional greenhouses, market gardens, a laundry, and poultry and dairy farms were completed. (Except for the Berkshire Hotel, which was demolished in the 1960s, and the original Village Hall, the main buildings of the village are still in existence.)

In the midst of this rapid growth, James Tufts made a discovery that had the potential to destroy the village. After the Holly Inn and several of the cottages had been built, Tufts learned that consumption was a contagious disease. Without patients to fill his rooms, he now feared he could not draw enough people to be successful. He needed another attraction.

The trolley came from Southern Pines and stopped directly in front of the Holly Inn. Its normal season ran from November until April. The Holly Inn was placed on the National Register of Historical Places in 1973 and is considered to be one of the finest examples of Victorian architecture.

Tufts had visited other health resorts and had found them less than adequate in terms of leisure activities. He had also noticed that many of his initial guests had brought golf clubs and balls with them and were playing the sport in a nearby pasture. In addition, the surrounding area offered abundant wildlife—making it ideal for hunting. A firm believer in the benefits of daily exercise (James was a fan of roque, a modified version of croquet), he soon saw a new reason to visit the village: outdoor sports.

There was another change. In order to protect the resort and the village, prospective guests would soon be required to produce a certificate of good health and a letter from a minister attesting to the guest's high moral character.

By mid-1896, the Holly Inn, two apartment houses, four boarding houses, and thirty-four cottages had been built. The demand for rooms was increasing rapidly, so the construction of the Carolina Hotel began in 1898.

The Carolina Hotel opened on January 1, 1901. It was a four-story Colonial Revival and the largest frame hotel in North Carolina. Its name was changed by the Diamondhead Corporation to the Pinehurst Hotel in 1973, but it was renamed the Carolina in 1998 by ClubCorp, its new owner. It was also expanded to 300 rooms.

The Music Room was located on the east side of the Carolina and was attached by a covered walkway. It held a large stage, dressing rooms, a dance floor, and seats for 500. It was used for concerts, parties, and other social events.

The Oak and Hanover Cottages were built in 1895. In the summer of 1898, the two cottages were combined to meet the increasing demand for accommodations in Pinehurst. The new building was called the Berkshire Hotel and was expanded in the summer of 1899. The rates were $2 per day or $10 and up for a week. The Berkshire was demolished in the summer of 1960.

The Magnolia Inn, on the corner of Chinquapin and Magnolia, opened in November 1897. It offered rooms for $8 to $12 per week. Originally used as an annex to the Holly Inn, it was located only steps from the general offices, the department store, the post office, and the library. In 1901 the inn's dining room and kitchen were enlarged. The Magnolia's rooms were large and airy, and there was a veranda on three sides.

For a brief period in the late 1940s, the Magnolia was used by Dr. Francis Owens as an office and surgery facility. In 1989 it was restored and reopened as a bed-and-breakfast.

Built by Emma Bliss in 1923, the Manor Inn had sixty guest rooms. It was built on the site of the Lexington, a hotel constructed by James Walker Tufts to house resort employees. It was four stories tall and built of red brick and Kellastone, a concrete material.

The Manor's roof was made of fireproof asbestos shingles. After sixty-seven years of existence and a variety of owners, it was purchased once again in 1990, this time by Resorts of Pinehurst, Inc.

The first schoolhouse was built at the foot of the Village Green. It was surrounded with playground areas and flowers, and its architect boasted that it had "the best system of ventilation in vogue." Parents were assured that their children "will receive educational advantages equal to those of their Northern homes."

By the middle of 1896, more than thirty cottages had been built. The early cottages were not mansions for the wealthy, but simple and well-built structures. In the summer of 1899, during an expansion of the Holly Inn, Charles D. Benbow, the first manager of Pinehurst, suggested moving the Holly's sunroom to the Pine Grove House. A glass corridor was then built between the Pine Grove and the relocated sunroom. Due to drafts caused by the large amount of glass, a stove was installed in the sunroom and a flue was run up through the roof.

The cottages were usually named for plants, flowers, or places in New England. Originally, the cottages were rented for the season at 10 percent of the cost to build them. Arlington Cottage, originally called Retreat, was built on Everette Road in 1895, about a half block from the Holly Inn.

Thirty-eight cottages were built between 1895 and 1897 (nearly thirty are still in existence). Mistletoe Cottage was built in 1895 and was the home of Leonard Tufts for many years. In 1912 it was relocated next to Mystic Cottage from its original location on Chinquapin Road.

The Casino (right) and Mistletoe Cottage, under construction in 1895.

The Casino operated from November 1 until June 1 and was open to all Pinehurst residents. The lower floor housed a Ladies' Parlor and Café. On the second floor there was a reading room (fully stocked with daily newspapers and popular periodicals), a billiard room, a smoking room, bathrooms, and a barber shop. Because many boarding houses and cottages did not have kitchens, the Casino Café offered three meals a day at $4.50 per week or just dinners for $2.50 per week. There was also a bakery in the Café where residents could purchase supplies.

When it was built in 1897, the Pinehurst Department Store was said to cover more square footage than any other store in Moore County. The center portion was used for groceries, hardware, and crockery. The post office, dry and fancy goods, clothing, drugs, stationery, and a circulating library were located on the left side. On the right side were the village office and the private offices of the resident manager and Leonard Tufts. The meat market and cold storage were in the basement. On the second floor were eleven rooms used as one- or two-bedroom suites. A large room in the rear was used as a photographic studio. Leonard is shown in front of the store in 1923.

As additional holes were built, the clubhouse expanded as well (shown here in 1900).

When guests took over the dairy farm and began chasing around a small white ball with clubs, it disturbed the dairy cattle. James Walker Tufts and the dairy manager were worried that milk production would suffer. Unable to dissuade guests from participating in this strange new activity, James had a nine-hole course built in 1898 that was designed by Dr. Leroy Culver of New York. By the end of 1899, the No. 1 course had been expanded to eighteen holes and a clubhouse was built, using plans that cost Tufts $15.

Frank Presbrey, a New York advertising executive hired by Pinehurst, came up with the idea of using golf tournaments to promote the area. The idea was so successful that an observation deck had to be added to accommodate spectators.

A beautiful (and often photographed) arched veranda was also added to the clubhouse.

The village was expanding as well. Deer Park was established on seven acres south of the Village Green and became the home to a herd of tame deer. There were also Chinese pheasants and Belgian hares. In November 1901 a group of guests and villagers held a ceremony to officially name each of the deer. One deer, named Sears Roebuck, wandered the village freely and was known to visit the library and several of the cottages. It was also frequently seen playing with children and dogs.

The Community House was built in 1914. A Community Hall Association was formed to handle the debt and expenses of the building and to do welfare work in the village. The villagers supported it through contributions. In 1920 the Presbyterian Church was organized, and it began using the Community House for morning Sunday School and Sunday evening services. The church rented the lower portion, and the Woodmen of the World rented the upper hall. The trustees had paid off the debt by the spring of 1921.

The Carolina Theater opened in February 1923 on the site of the old printing office. The building was made of terra cotta patterned brick and stucco, and had a green Spanish-style tile roof and a hexagonal shape. The cost of the building was approximately $50,000.

Located at the east side of the Village Green, a short distance from the Holly Inn, the Village Hall was used for nondenominational Sunday services. The building had a capacity of 300 and featured a fifteen-by-twenty-foot stage. It also offered ladies' and gentlemen's dressing rooms.

The Village Hall opened its doors for the first time on Christmas Day in 1897. After the Religious Association of Pinehurst purchased it in 1908, the hall became the first Village Chapel. A steeple was later added. A completely new chapel was constructed in 1924.

The Pine Crest Inn opened on February 5, 1913. The owners, Henry and Emma Bliss, had come from New Hampshire in 1903 to operate the Lexington Hotel. In 1921 the Pine Crest Inn was sold to Donald Ross and close friend James MacNab. A few years later, Ross and MacNab built another wing. In 1948, the year of his death, Ross sold the Pine Crest to Carl Moser, former general manager of the Carolina Hotel in Chapel Hill.

This early photograph shows the intersection of Chinquapin Road and Magnolia Road. Mystic Cottage is on the left, and Mistletoe Cottage is in the center. The strip of plantings between the street and the buildings was a public area, a trait of Frederick Law Olmsted's designs.

The intersection of Community Road and Orange Road. Reading clockwise, the building at the lower left is the old Community House. The large white building at upper left is the Fire Department, and the small dark roof to the right of it is Arcadia Cottage. Thistle Cottage is next, then Afterglow Cottage and its garage.

The Chalfonte was a small elegant hotel located about a mile south of Pinehurst that opened on November 20, 1927. Situated on ten acres, it offered thirty rooms. During World War II, the Chalfonte was leased to a group of army officers and their families who were stationed at Fort Bragg, North Carolina. After the war it became a popular nightspot, offering varied types of live entertainment. In 1951 it was converted into the Pinehurst Convalescent Center. A patient's family or friends could visit and spend the night in one of the public rooms. Traces of the driveways, landscaping, and crumbled walls are all that remain today.

A view up Market Street toward the Holly Inn. The Wellesley Building housed Wallace's Dry Goods and Apparel and the Moore County Beverage store, circa late 1930s or early 1940s.

The cornerstone of the Sacred Heart Catholic Church was laid in 1919, but the church was not dedicated until 1921. Catholic services were held in the Old Village Hall until the congregation grew too large. The building was brick with a stucco-covered foundation, and it featured a gabled and timbered entrance and a slender spire. A new, larger church was built in 1994.

The first meeting of the Women's Exchange was held on May 2, 1923. The original members traveled the county and taught neighbors how to sew, knit, crochet, hook and braid rugs, bake, and make jams and jellies. They also sold their homemade goods. The building they met in had originally been constructed in 1823 by James Ray and had served as the family kitchen.

James Walker Tufts purchased the Exchange building and had it moved to the village to serve as the Pinehurst Museum. In a letter to Richard S. Tufts, Rassie Wicker, a village historian, cartographer, and former fire chief, said that the exhibits consisted mostly of some petrified wood and "an enormous key said to have been from the lock on the Fayetteville jail, or more likely, from the old armory which [Union General H. Judson] Kilpatrick burned during the Civil War." The building was expanded in 1928. In 1957, ladies opened a tea room for serving light luncheons.

The Pinehurst Steam Laundry opened in 1898. Bundles were dropped off at the General Store. In 1899 a two-story, fifty-foot addition was built on the east side of the existing laundry. The second floor held eight rooms for the use of the employees.

The Pinehurst Poultry Farm was started in 1902, and within two years it grew to be one of the largest in the south. Its major purpose was to provide the village with roasting chickens, broilers, and capons. In 1903 the farm began breeding fancy poultry: duck, turkey, geese, quail, and pheasant. The farms were always open to the guests and the most popular attractions were the poultry incubators. Eggs were exhibited in every stage of development day and night, and "birthday parties" were announced regularly and attended by the guests.

Tufts knew that in order to fill the needs of his guests he would require a farm and a dairy. One hundred acres on the south side of the village were selected and cleared. The barn had two stories and a basement. It accommodated thirty head of beef and dairy cattle and storage for fodder and farm implements. A spring near the barn provided fresh water. A few hundred yards from the dairy was a piggery stocked with well-bred Berkshires, and in a nearby pasture there were sheep and goats. Also on the property was a small cottage built for the farmer in charge. In 1903 the Pinehurst Dairy produced 200 gallons of milk every day from Holstein, Jersey, and Ayrshire cattle. By 1910 it was considered the only modern dairy in North Carolina.

The Market Garden supplied vegetables for guests as well as the hotels. The greenhouses were filled with lettuce, radishes, cauliflower, beets, carrots, dandelions, Brussels sprouts, spinach, cucumbers, celery—even mushrooms and kohlrabi. One of the more important functions of the gardens and greenhouses was to find a solution to the lawn-grass problem, because growing grass was a challenge in the sandy soil and hot, humid climate. Originally begun to supplement the village plantings, the greenhouses developed into a commercial enterprise, selling plantings to northern parks and gardens.

By 1895 nine acres of land had been cleared about a mile outside of the village boundary and were readied for the plantings that were arriving from nurseries nearby and as far away as France. By January 1896 the greenhouses were expanded to twenty acres because more vegetable gardens were needed. During summers, cuttings were made and seeds were harvested to continue propagation of the trees and shrubberies. In the nursery, guests were given the opportunity to pick cotton, dig peanuts, and even smoke Pinehurst-grown tobacco.

In the earliest days of Pinehurst, goods, construction materials, and guests were transported by horse-drawn wagons. The Pinehurst Livery Stable, shown here in 1901, was built in 1898. Originally, the livery accommodated twenty-five horses, paddocks, a carriage shed, an owl, and a family of possums. There were water and toilets and a washing area for carriages. Horses boarded for $4 per week.

Due to an increasing number of motor vehicles in Pinehurst, Leonard Tufts built a garage in 1910. By July, more than thirty spaces had been reserved for the 1910–1911 season. In February 1913 a new workshop was built that was the equal of any in the state. The upper floor held apartments for the garage manager. Part of the garage still stands and is in use as a car dealership.

In 1898 a dangerous forest fire threatened the village. Pine trees that had been left behind by the turpentine industry were dead, dry, and loaded with flammable resins. The conflagration was aided by raging winds, and fires quickly broke out in sight of the village. Firefighters (local residents) were sent into the woods to protect the village. Fire Chief Rassie Wicker is shown seated on a horse-drawn fire wagon.

In the spring of 1899, an electric fire alarm system with fifteen fireboxes was completed. The Power House was equipped with a pressure hydrant system, hose wagon, and a huge pump. Chief Wicker is shown with a fire extinguisher on the left and a hose cart on the right, both horse-drawn. The equipment was kept in the basement of the department store.

The Amphidrome, or Fair Barn, was erected in 1917 to be used as the Agriculture Hall for the Moore County Fair, which was famed throughout the southeast. The walls were lined with jars of fruits and vegetables on exhibit. As equestrian sports became more popular, the fair was moved from Pinehurst and the exhibit building became a stable with an indoor arena. Between 1932 and 1992, the track property was a harness training facility.

In October 1932 a tornado touched down in Pinehurst. The Fair Barn was severely damaged by winds that tore off most of the slate roof, two of the four cupolas, and the glass skylight. Subsequent repairs were made to keep the building in use as a stable, but it was not until 1998 that sufficient private and public funds were raised to completely restore the Fair Barn. At a cost of over a million dollars, it was returned to an open exhibit area with 7,400 square feet of space. It is the oldest surviving exhibition barn in the state.

Water was first supplied to the village in 1895. There were three wells: one in front of the Theater Building, one near the Power House, and one near the future location of the Carolina Hotel. By 1911, nine wells had been drilled. Pressure was obtained through a 54-foot tank located behind the Casino. When the Carolina Hotel was built, a small water tank was installed in the cupola to provide adequate water pressure for the guests.

The Power House, built in 1896, was the village's only source of power until well into the 1950s. The steam power plant provided heat and electricity for the hotels, cottages, businesses, and trolleys. The trolley cars were also stored there. In 1903 duplicate machinery was installed as a backup in case of emergency. After the smokestack had to be removed in 1999, the Power House continued to fall into disrepair. In 2002, the Pinehurst Village Council approved its demolition.

In the days when the village was first being built, many of the local residents worked as farmhands. Like several of the surrounding communities, Moore County was suffering from economic distress. Workers are shown in the process of drying peanuts after harvest. Peanuts were not a major crop in the Sandhills, but were probably planted to help improve the sandy soil.

Chapter 3

LIFE IN THE VILLAGE

When James Walker Tufts purchased the land that would become his village, the town of Southern Pines had already been established as a health resort and tourist attraction. The Ozone Hotel, where Tufts lived while Pinehurst was being built, had been in business since 1892.

Pinehurst's construction created a large need for laborers. Many black men in the area picked fruit or cotton or had jobs in the turpentine industry, and many black women worked in area homes or hotels. Since some of the men also had experience in bricklaying and masonry, the growing village became another source of employment.

Initially, a large number of construction workers had come from northern states. Many of the doormen and carriage drivers would come from the north as well. Local laborers were also employed, however, often clearing land, carrying supplies, building roads, or driving mule carts. Eventually, when the northern workers returned home, local residents filled their jobs. In order to staff his hotels with servers and other workers, Tufts ran ads in northern newspapers for "Irish Catholic girls." He had visited the resort of Wentworth-by-the-Sea in Rhode Island and had been impressed by the staff's service and efficiency. In time, he would arrange for Wentworth's staff to come to Pinehurst for the winter season. The following March or April, when Pinehurst closed for the summer, the staff would return home to work at Wentworth.

Additional jobs became available as each new building was completed—the greenhouses, the market gardens, the poultry farms, and the dairy all needed workers. Nothing, however, did more to improve the lot of the local black population than the introduction of golf.

The suddenly booming golf industry gave local blacks the opportunity to work for better money and benefits. In the early days of golf at Pinehurst, the caddies were of all ages, and even the very young could find work. They rode to the course on the trolley and were served meals. While waiting for their next bag, they entertained the players by singing and dancing. In later years, there was even a caddie band. (In 1925, Mrs. Leonard Tufts became concerned because young children were caddying instead of going to school. Consequently, she arranged for a bus to take them to school and then return them to the club afterward for work. Eventually, only children that had reached the age of sixteen were allowed to caddie.)

One of the advantages of the climate in the Sandhills was that it was particularly well suited to growing peaches. The North Carolina Department of Agriculture reported that "peaches grown in this area have an unusually fine flavor, and are particularly good shippers." In 1898, 670 tons of fruit, mostly peaches, were shipped out from Southern Pines.

When the construction of Pinehurst began in1895, almost all supplies, goods, workers, and visitors were carried there from Southern Pines via schooner wagons or horse-drawn trolleys. The wagons had wide wheels that prevented them from sinking into the soft sand of the trail that eventually would become Midland Road. Farmers and other purveyors of goods also drove their wagons to the village, to sell goods at the department store. It was usually a long and dusty ride, and Leonard eventually became aware of the drawback that the trip presented to the village. He understood the connection between timely and comfortable travel and the economic success of his father's venture. (He would later become a strong advocate of better roads throughout the state of North Carolina.) In an attempt to create a hard surface, Leonard began experimenting with mixing clay from a nearby pit into the sandy trail.

It wasn't long before electric-powered trolleys were replacing horse-drawn trolleys, and a seven-mile line was then built between Southern Pines and Pinehurst. The track ran in front of the Holly Inn and on toward the department store. The trolley was primarily for passengers, but it also carried goods if there was extra room. After the Carolina Hotel was built, the track was extended around to the back of the structure. During peak season, the trolley constantly ran between Southern Pines and Pinehurst, making as many as seven trips per day. The cars were open or closed, dependent upon the weather, and could even be heated by electricity when the temperature dropped. Because of extended stays by many of the guests, extra cars were often needed to carry the large amounts of luggage.

On December 17, 1903, in Kitty Hawk, North Carolina, Orville Wright made man's first flight. The trip was all of 120 feet long, lasting twelve seconds. Later in the day, with brother Wilbur at the controls, a second flight lasted fifty-nine seconds and traveled 852 feet. Amazingly, less than a decade later, Pinehurst not only had a flying field (actually, a dairy field) but its own resident stunt flyer, flight teacher, and flight service. When Chick Evans won the North and South Amateur in 1911, he was given the dubious prize of a ride above the village in a flying machine.

Not many years later, visitors were flying to Pinehurst from all over the country.

One of the Ayrshire cows at the dairy farm was named Tootsie Mitchell and was the head of a line of fine specimens. The Ayrshires were chosen for their strength in breeding and for the large quantities of milk they produced.

In 1895 razorback hogs were commonly raised in the area. James Walker Tufts, however, wanted Berkshire hogs. They were quick to mature, required less feed, and bore large litters. Berkshires were the only pure-bred hogs in the state of North Carolina and were located in Asheville, at the Biltmore Estate. The Pinehurst hogs were purchased from the Vanderbilt herd.

The Pinehurst hogs were wellbred, wellfed, and good breeders. James' son, Leonard, kept meticulous records on scientific breeding and improvement of livestock. He believed that a poor breeder ate as much as a good breeder. They even sponsored an annual "Pinehurst Pig Feeding Contest." The piggery furnished the pigs, and local boys would care for them for a 150-day feeding period. The pigs with the largest weight gain earned their caretakers cash prizes of $35 donated by Richard Tufts. Donald Ross also donated a prize of $25 to the boy with the largest, most economical gain and the best cost record.

North Carolina was a free-range territory at the time the village was growing. Because of the roaming animals, including wild razorback hogs, a tall wire fence was built around the village. The hogs often got in, however, and would be found rooting around fresh plantings. Hogs also slipped beneath cottages and rubbed their bristly, hairy backs against the floorboards, much to the dismay of the residents. There was a stiff penalty for leaving a gate open ($50) but it was rarely collected. Gates were erected at several spots around the village. The trolley from Southern Pines entered a gate behind the Carolina, and people in wagons or on horseback were forced to dismount to enter or exit. Woe be it to anybody who failed to properly close a gate!

Many local residents worked as farm-hands, turpentine workers, masons, and bricklayers. They also cleared land and built roads. Soon, though, the growing village offered a new occupation—caddying.

Around the turn of the twentieth century, many of the female residents of Moore County were working in households and local hotels.

At first, caddies were of all ages, and many were recruited from the school in Taylortown. In 1925 Leonard's wife Gertrude became concerned that too many youngsters were caddying instead of going to school. She arranged for a bus to take them to school and then drop them off at the club for work. Before long, a new rule stated that caddies had to be sixteen years of age.

Caddying became a good way to make a decent wage. In this photograph from 1923, caddies wait in line for dinner outside the Department Store. It was not until 1926 that golf was permitted on Sunday, and then only in the afternoon.

Pinehurst caddies waiting for assignments near the clubhouse.

Three veteran Pinehurst caddies: Thomas Franklin Dowd,
Ed Gaines, and John Henry
Dowd. Ed Gaines caddied for
four generations of Tufts.

Joe Milton was an unusual villager. He lived on Chicken Plant Road about a mile and a half west of the Carolina. He was a folk artist and used his home and his yard as his canvas. His property was covered in hand-lettered signs and drawings. During the day, he rode around in his wagon and scavenged garbage for his hogs, tended fires for people in the village, and gave rides in his oxcart.

Tom Cotton was born in 1843 and began life as a slave. After he eventually gained his freedom he had several jobs, including a fifteen-year stretch with the railroad. He moved to Pinehurst in 1913.

Tom and a few of his friends are shown here with some opossums they caught. In addition to working as a caddie, Tom did all manner of odd jobs around the club. When Tom was no longer able to caddie, he became a groundskeeper and worked for the resort until his death in 1928. He was so beloved that an employee golf tournament was named after him.

Midland Road was the main route between Southern Pines and Pinehurst. Construction materials, produce, and goods arrived by train in Southern Pines and were then transported to Pinehurst. The route consisted of soft, deep sand, and schooner wagons were necessary to travel the six-mile distance. In the early days it was a difficult and lengthy trip. When he moved to Pinehurst after his father died, Leonard Tufts began to understand how important good roads would be to the economy and success of the village. He experimented with mixing clay into the sandy trail and eventually created a hard surface. When the resurfacing was completed, a celebration was held and community leaders from Southern Pines and Pinehurst were given rides to demonstrate its superiority. Midland Road was divided in 1939 and today is one of the oldest four-lane divided roads in the state.

Opposite: Demus Taylor was another highly respected Pinehurst worker. In the days that Demus worked in the turpentine industry, he was famed for being able to "cut the box" on a tree in ten minutes, using his own special seven-pound axe. Demus and his son Robert bought land outside of Pinehurst in the early 1900s and sold lots to create the neighboring burg of Taylortown.

In 1895 James Walker Tufts and the New England Mining, Manufacturing and Estate Company entered into an agreement, for the price of $1, to establish a right-of-way for an electric railway alongside the Seaboard Air Line Railroad in Southern Pines. Until the electric trolley was established, a horse-drawn trolley brought guests to Pinehurst. The tracks ran right in front of the Holly Inn. By 1897, the trolley line was seven miles long. Customers could travel first class if they wished, and the cars could be open or closed. In cold weather, the cars were heated by electricity. A trip between Southern Pines and Pinehurst cost fifteen cents.

The Pinehurst depot was located near the Carolina. The name of the stop in Southern Pines became known as "Pinehurst Junction," which caused some hard feelings between the communities until the trolley line was closed in 1905. The trolley continued to operate within the village for two more years.

These open cars were used to carry goods, construction materials, and the extra luggage needed to accommodate the extended stays of many of the guests.

During the season, special cars were added to the trains destined for the Village of Pinehurst. Many of the cars were private, such as the one shown here, hired by the H. B. Swoope family. Swoope was a Pennsylvania banker with extensive property holdings in Pinehurst and was instrumental in the success of the Village Chapel.

Causey Talbert came to the Pinehurst Garage Company in 1919, and was employed there until his death in 1963. In 1926 Talbert was given the assignment of driving "Miss Carolina" to and from the Pinehurst Country Club and the hotel, plus trips to Southern Pines. Guests and residents soon christened him "Happy" due to his ever-present grin and cheerfulness. Hap and "Miss Carolina" served Pinehurst for forty years. He was so appreciated that when his home was destroyed by fire in 1943, members of the country club contributed enough money to build a new home for Causey and his wife and ten children.

At the outbreak of World War II, Lloyd Yost enlisted as an aviator in the Signal Corps. By 1919, he was Post Adjutant. In 1926 he was offered the WACO plane agency in North Carolina and chose Pinehurst as his base, using the dairy pasture as a landing field. In 1927 Yost moved his operations to the Knollwood Airfield after being reprimanded by Leonard Tufts.

Tufts was quoted in the *Pinehurst Outlook* as saying, "I think more of the cows than I do of the airplanes. And airplanes have got to go."

This Pinehurst Flying Field booklet, where Lloyd O. Yost was the Transport Pilot Manager, boasted "The fare for a short hop over Pinehurst is $2.50." For short hops, WACO biplanes with Curtis OX5 motors were used. On longer journeys, Fairchild Cabin Monoplanes were used with the Wright Whirlwind Motor. Fares to Raleigh, Greensboro, or Florence, South Carolina were $100 round-trip. In the late 1930s, round-trip to New York for four passengers was $600.

Lincoln Beechy, who also flew at Pinehurst, was a famous aviator from the Midwest. He performed stunts as well as delivered goods and services. He is shown here at Pinehurst Field with Commander S. Saito of the Japanese Navy (circa 1910).

Amelia Earhart made several visits to Pinehurst with her husband George Putnam. Her first trip to Knollwood Airport was on November 13, 1931. She arrived in her autogyro plane that was sponsored by the Beech-Nut Chewing Gum Company.

Chapter 4

DONALD ROSS AND THE GROWTH OF GOLF

The game of golf sneaked into Pinehurst on the backs of guests who couldn't leave it behind. Suddenly, it seemed, small white balls were being knocked around the dairy fields. Fearing for the safety of his prized Ayrshire cattle and the large amount of milk they produced, Tufts decided to relocate the golfers by providing a playing area. During the 1897-1898 season, he commissioned a nine-hole course to be built on sixty acres south of the Village Green. Dr. Leroy Culver, a New York native who had visited many of the finest courses in England and Scotland and was then living in Southern Pines, laid out the course. John Dunn Tucker was then given a contract to be the course superintendent and golf instructor. By the fall of the following year, a clubhouse had been built and the course had been expanded to eighteen holes. In March 1900 three-time British Open champion Harry Vardon visited Pinehurst and was impressed with both the area and the golf. Later that year, at his summer home in Massachusetts, Tufts hired a new golf pro for Pinehurst. His name was Donald Ross.

Donald James Ross was born in Dornoch, Scotland, on November 23, 1872. His father, Murdoch, was a stonemason. At age fourteen, Donald became a carpenter's apprentice under master carpenter Peter Murray. He also began to caddie at the local golf links. In 1893 Donald moved to St. Andrews to apprentice under "Old Tom" Morris, a well-known clubmaker and greenkeeper and the professional at the town's famous "Old Course."

In early 1899, while continuing to progress as a greenkeeper, clubmaker, and golfer, Ross met a Harvard University professor on holiday in Scotland who was a member of Oakley Country Club in Watertown, Massachusetts. Impressed by Ross' skill at the game and aware that golf was booming back home, the professor urged Donald to move to America.

Donald James Ross was born in Dornoch, Scotland, in 1872. He became a carpenter's apprentice at age fourteen and also began to caddie at the Dornoch links. Later he moved to St. Andrews to learn clubmaking and green-keeping under Old Tom Morris. In 1899 he came to America and made the acquaintance of James Walker Tufts, who was in search of a golf professional for Pinehurst. In 1900 Ross accepted a job from Mr. Tufts to work the winter season.

Donald Ross, Francis Ouimet (1913 U.S. Open champion), Alex Ross (Donald's brother and club pro in Boston and Detroit), and Jack Jolly, a ball manufacturer from New Jersey and a Pinehurst regular.

Ross headed to the United States that spring and quickly became employed at Oakley Country Club. It was while at Oakley that Ross met James Walker Tufts. In the summer of 1900 Tufts offered Ross the job of head professional at Pinehurst during the winter season. Ross accepted and continued to work at Oakley from spring to late fall. In addition to his duties as the golf pro, Ross reworked the existing eighteen holes and, as demand grew, added nine more holes in 1901. Three years later, Ross returned to Scotland and came back with a bride. In December 1904 he married Janet Kennedy Conchie, an avid golfer. Their only child (named Lillian after Donald's mother) was born in 1910.

The Tin Whistles were a group of male golfers who were winter residents. Organized in 1904, the group originally met at the Holly Inn. At the tenth hole of the No. 1 course, thirsty gentlemen could blow a whistle and someone would emerge from the woods with scotch that could be mixed with water from a nearby spring. The Tin Whistle springhouse was made of twisted knots and cypress slabs. The Tin Whistles, still active as a golf and civic club, celebrated their 100th anniversary in 2004. A similar club for women, the Silver Foils, was founded in 1909. Its purpose was to promote friendly games and good sportsmanship. The Silver Foils are also still active as a golf and civic group. (Donald Ross is sitting to the left at the top of the stairs).

One evening in early January 1906, a number of gentlemen at the Holly Inn remarked on the brilliance of the moonlight on the sandy soil. One even speculated that it was bright enough to play a golf match. A plan was soon hatched, a $40 purse was raised, and Jack Jolly persuaded Donald Ross to play. On January 9, the sky was cloudless and the moon was full and brilliant on the sand. Talk of the match had spread and by the time it started, at 8 p.m., there was a gallery of nearly 200 spectators. The only deviation from the regular rules of golf was the use of several fore caddies to assist in locating the balls. Each player sacrificed distance for accuracy and not a single ball was lost. Putting proved to be troublesome because the holes were difficult to see. In just over two hours the match was over, with Ross the victor over Jolly, 5 and 4.

Ross met his second wife, Florence Sturgie Blackinton, when he was sent to assess her cottage in Pinehurst. They became close and were married in 1924. Ross moved into the cottage and they named it Dornoch, after his beloved homeland. Donald and Florence were unable to agree on a design style so they compromised. The front resembled a Scottish cottage, the back looked like a Southern mansion. Ross enjoyed gardening and planted beautiful roses and shrubbery around Dornoch Cottage. Dornoch remained his home until his death in April 1948.

Construction of the early golf courses at Pinehurst was all done by hand, with horse- and mule-drawn carts, wagons, and apparatuses. Using a variation of a road-building tool called the King Road Drag, workers created the fairways that generally followed the lay of the land. An adjustable blade was then used to smooth the ground, and bunkers were dug out with a drag pan. All the holes at Pinehurst had sand greens that were rolled each morning and sprinkled with water that was carried in barrels on wagons. Sometimes a mixture of clay and oil was added. The moisture evaporated quickly and left a surface much like that of a billiard table. After play on a green was completed, a caddie would drag a piece of carpet across the surface and smooth it for the players coming along next. Nearly forty years would go by before Pinehurst had greens made of grass.

A second eighteen-hole course, the now famous No. 2 (designed by Ross), opened in 1907. For the average player, No. 2 was considered very challenging and an excellent course for tournament play. That same year an additional nine holes were built. In 1910 the No. 3 course opened, offering fewer hazards and wider fairways to suit the less-skillful players who simply wished to enjoy a round of golf.

In 1919 Janet Ross was diagnosed with breast cancer. She never recovered and died on February 12, 1922, at Hawthorne cottage, the Ross residence from 1914 to 1922. Lillian was twelve years old.

As the village and hotels grew, so did the demand for golf. Nine more holes were built, intended for employees of the resort. These "holes" were soon relinquished to the needs of the guests and country club members. Nine more were added and combined in 1923 to create the No. 4 course. All four courses were designed or reworked by Ross.

Donald and Florence were both widowed when they met in 1924. This photo was taken twelve years later. They were married for twenty-four years when Donald died. Florence survived until 1955.

It was also in 1923 that Ross met Florence Sturgie Blackinton at her cottage near the third green at Pinehurst No. 2. Both had lost a spouse, and they were quickly drawn to each other. They married in 1924, and Ross moved into her home, renaming it Dornoch Cottage. Florence also had a home in Little Compton, Rhode Island, where Ross spent the off-season. During the time that Ross was managing the courses at Pinehurst, he was also establishing a successful, nationwide business designing golf courses. His influence and prestige continued to grow both in and out of Pinehurst and he became a vital part of the thriving resort.

For years, Ross had searched for a grass that would grow on Pinehurst's greens and survive the heat and humidity of the summer. In 1934 he and his course superintendent, Frank Maples, began experimenting with bermudagrass and finally gained some success. More greens were planted on Pinehurst No. 2 in 1935, and by 1936, in time to host the PGA Championship, all of its greens were grassed. A few years later, all of the greens on all of the courses at Pinehurst were grass.

Throughout his long and illustrious career, Donald Ross designed nearly 400 golf courses. In truth, however, there were many that he never even saw. He designed them by using topographical maps as guides and by offering detailed instructions to trusted associates and course contractors. In 1916 Ross hired course architect J. B. McGovern and created the firm of Donald Ross & Associates. Two years later Donald hired Walter B. Hatch, a landscape architect and engineer. His associates made on-site visits and supervised construction while Ross was busy in

Ross is shown in front of the first clubmaker's shop on the No. 3 course in the mid-1930s. Included in the group are R. Hewitt Swope of Merion Country Club (winner of the St. Valentine's Tournament), Glenna Collett Vare (U.S. Women's Amateur champion), Norman Maxwell (winner of the 1917 North and South Amateur), and Frank Maples (Pinehurst course superintendent).

Pinehurst. In 1920 Ross added Walter Irving Johnson Jr., another engineer, to his staff. It was Johnson who had the ability to create technical yet beautiful drawings, finally lending depth and scale to Ross' simple renditions. Another important employee was Eric Nelson. He worked for Ross in the capacity of personal assistant or secretary from his teens until Ross' retirement in 1946, and then succeeded him as club manager at Pinehurst Country Club. Ross' amazing body of work exists, in part, because of his ability to recognize talent and his loyal and hard-working employees.

On April 25, 1948, Donald James Ross suffered a heart attack and was taken to Moore Regional Hospital in Pinehurst. He died the next day at the age of seventy-five. Following his funeral in the Village Chapel, he was buried next to his first wife, Janet, in New Centre, Massachusetts. When Florence died in 1955, she was buried next to her first husband.

Donald Ross and caddie
on the seventh hole of
the No. 3 course.

Ross approaching a green
on the No. 4 course
(circa 1927).

Ross putting on a sand green in 1935. Some greens had already been seeded with bermudagrass in anticipation of the 1936 PGA Championship.

Ross enjoyed pleasant relations with the employees of the resort. Here he is chatting with the caddie master Jack Williams at the Pinehurst Country Club caddie shack.

Donald Ross and his employees in 1931. Back row, left to right: Ellis Maples, James MacNab, Joe Capello, Roy Bromson, Tom Naile, Clarence Lyman, Donald Currie, George McLeod, William Agnew, Jack Williams, Ted Turner, True Cheney, John Fitzgerald. Front Row, left to right: John Capello, Eric Nelson, Bert Nicoll, Ross, Frank Maples, William Wilson, Alexander Innes, Aneas Ross, Mr. (unknown) Mitchell.

Leonard Tufts and Ross in 1926. Leonard had been at the helm of the resort for nearly twenty-five years, and Pinehurst had four Ross-designed courses.

Richard Tufts and Ross were instrumental in the success of golf at Pinehurst. Ross continued to improve the Pinehurst courses, particularly No. 2, for the rest of his life, experimenting with grass greens, improving turf, and making adjustments as the game and equipment evolved. Richard played an important role in golf in Pinehurst, but also worldwide. He helped refine the rules of the game, was president of the USGA from 1956 to 1957, and promoted good sportsmanship and gentlemanly conduct.

It's said that Ross dearly loved his Packard. Most likely this is a posed photo for an advertisement. The Pinehurst Country Club clubhouse is in the background.

In 1920, while managing the Pinehurst golf courses and running a successful golf course design business, Ross and his close friend James MacNab purchased the Pine Crest Inn from Henry and Emma Bliss. The Pine Crest, just around the corner from the Holly Inn, was for a time the only privately owned hotel in Pinehurst.

The Pine Crest Inn had forty rooms, a dining room, a cozy fireplace, and a large veranda. While Ross was busy with his other responsibilities, MacNab handled the day-to-day operations of the inn. In 1923 Ross and MacNab added another wing.

Ross prepares to hit his drive on the eleventh hole (currently the tenth hole) at Pine Needles Golf Club in Southern Pines, another of Ross' designs. The eleventh is a dogleg to the left, and the tee shot must carry a small water hazard. W. E. Truesdell stands to the right.

On April 25, 1948, Ross suffered a heart attack and was taken to Moore Memorial Hospital in Pinehurst. He died there the next day at age seventy-five. His funeral was in the Pinehurst Village Chapel, and he was buried at the side of his first wife, Janet, in New Centre, Massachusetts.

In the early days of Pinehurst, before golf was established there, guests brought their own balls and clubs and played in the dairy fields.

As golf became more popular at Pinehurst, more holes were needed. The work was done by hand with mule- or horse-drawn wagons and equipment.

Handmade equipment was used to pull tree stumps out of the ground.

After trees were cut and removed from fairways, drag boards were used to flatten the ground. Some of the equipment that was used was actually designed for road building.

Even with specially designed scoop pans, the creation of bunkers took much hard work.

In the early days of golf, sand from a "tee box" was formed into a small tower on which to place a ball. The tee boxes were kept full of sand by course workers.

All Pinehurst courses had sand greens until 1934, when they began experimenting with grasses. They were large and square-shaped, mainly to accommodate the machinery that was used.

The sand greens were kept watered to keep them firm. Sometimes a little oil or clay was mixed with the sand to harden the surface. Water was carried around the course in wooden barrels on horse-drawn wagons. Sometimes the barrels were sunk into the ground near the green.

When play on a green was completed, a caddie would pull a piece of carpet across the sand to smooth it for the next group of golfers.

Horse-drawn greensroller

Later, a steam-driven greens-roller was used to smooth the sand surfaces as well as large portions of the course.

To protect the fairways from being damaged by hooves, horses and mules wore boots during mowing. The inside measurement fit a specific size horseshoe. In 1900 a set of horse boots cost $12.

A group of avid golfers formed a club called the "Tin Whistles" in 1904. During play, they would stop at the Tin Whistle Spring for a wee nip.

Ladies on the links
(circa 1915).

Many of Pinehurst's first
caddies were very young.

EXPECTANTLY WAITING FOR THEIR PAY
AFTER A ROUND ON THE GOLF LINKS

Caddies often were able to hitch a ride to work on the trolley.

Jack Williams, caddie master, Eric Thompson, Elbert Currie, and Ed Gaines, caddie to four generations of Tufts. Gaines was over eighty when this shot was taken in 1944

When it opened in 1898, the No. 1 course was probably not much better than a cow pasture.

Spectators watch a ladies'
match at the twelfth on the
No. 1 course. Originally a
nine-hole layout, it was
expanded to eighteen holes
by John Dunn Tucker
(Pinehurst's golf professional
at the time) in 1899.

While on a whirlwind exhibition tour of America at the turn of the century, three-time British Open champion Harry Vardon visited Pinehurst. Here he is lining up a putt on the ninth green of the No. 1 course in March 1900.

When the first courses at Pinehurst were being built, hundreds of large rocks were unearthed. Many were deemed impractical to remove, so they were stacked, covered with topsoil, and turned into hazards called "pyramids" or "chocolate drops." This photo of some of these hazards appeared in the January 31, 1902, issue of the *Pinehurst Outlook*. Usually about waist high, the mounds were common on the No. 1 course and on the first nine of No. 2.

The early days of golf in Pinehurst featured open landscape, sand greens, and scrub pines.

This often photographed bent pine tree stood at the first hole on the No. 3 course, built in 1910. It is now the second hole.

In spite of the fashion of the day, ladies could still produce a high, balanced finish.

Spectators surround the eighteenth green on the No. 2 course during a competition in 1929.

Players make their way to the par-3 seventh green on No. 2. The faces of the bunkers at back left are much higher than they are today.

In 1932 the fourteenth green on No. 3 is still sand, as is much of the course itself.

The thirteenth green on No. 2 before the greens were changed from sand to grass in anticipation of the 1936 PGA Championship

Workers at the sundial green (for many years the practice green) appear to be hand-planting grass. They were also known to hand-cut crowfoot-grass weeds with knives.

The new grass green on the eleventh hole of No. 2 was in use by October 1935.

Once the greens had grass, they had to be mowed.

This is the Cathedral Hole (the fifteenth on the No. 5 course) during the
Women's North and South Amateur in the mid-thirties.

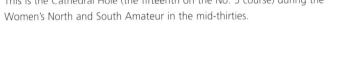

Another shot of the fifteenth on No. 5 (circa 1935). "Cathedral" is the only hole at Pinehurst that has a name.

Spectators encircle a green on the No. 2 course during play at the 1937 North and South Open.

Pinehurst's practice area (shown here in 1938) has long been known as "Maniac Hill."

A group prepares to tee off at the par-3 ninth hole on the No. 2 course. Considering Ross' continuous tinkering with No. 2, the ninth today is remarkably unchanged from its original design.

Sam Snead's legendary suppleness and wide shoulder turn are clearly evident as he tees off on the third hole at No. 2 during a North and South Open. Behind Snead is Paul Runyan.

Ben Hogan putts on the third green at No. 2 during the 1951 Ryder Cup at Pinehurst.

As golf became more popular, golfers of all ages began working on their games.

The frequent golf tournaments at Pinehurst always drew plenty of interested spectators

Frank Presbrey was the owner of a successful New York advertising agency that was retained in 1901 to promote Pinehurst. Presbrey became convinced that golf was the way to promote the village and that tournament play was the key to getting people to visit. The first tournament that he started at Pinehurst was called the Inaugural (later renamed the Mid-Winter).

Chapter 5
TOURNAMENT GOLF

In 1901 the Frank Presbrey Company, an advertising agency in New York City, was retained to promote the village of Pinehurst. The agency's owner was a regular visitor to Pinehurst, and he immediately began publicizing the village as a winter vacation spot and sports and recreation center. Presbrey was also aware that Harry Vardon had played golf in Pinehurst the year before and that he had written to James Tufts to say that "I have enjoyed playing on your course immensely … and in my judgment [it is] one which will compare very favorably with any of the Eastern courses."

Presbrey was sure that golf would be a very attractive and profitable pursuit. In the process of promoting the sport at Pinehurst, he also created the famous "golf lad" for his ads. The figure, which eventually evolved into today's famed Putter Boy, soon began appearing on menus, calendars, and other objects. His ads portrayed a land with beautiful skies, mild winters, healing pine ozone, and plenty of golf and other recreational activities. Presbrey's promotional pieces called Pinehurst "the healthiest, most perfect resort in the South." He also realized that by conducting tournaments at the resort he would attract more golfers. This was because the results of tournaments were often reported in newspapers, and everybody enjoyed reading about themselves and seeing their photos in the newspaper. Tournament photos and stories were also sent to newspapers in the north, and that helped attract even more golfers to the area.

Presbrey created the "golf lad" as a symbol for Pinehurst and used it extensively in ads for the village. Eventually evolving into Pinehurst's famous "Putter Boy," the golf lad was also used on menus, calendars, and other promotional pieces.

James G. Batterson was the winner of the first annual tournament for the members of the American Golf Association for Advertisers. Like several other Pinehurst tournaments, it was started by Frank Presbrey.

The North and South Amateur was started in 1901, the original Inaugural Tournament (later called the Mid-Winter Tournament) began in 1903, and an annual event for the American Golf Association for Advertisers began in 1905. Presbrey encouraged golfers of all abilities and even held a tournament (with a handsome silver trophy for the winner) for players who could not shoot less than 100 over eighteen holes. Not surprisingly, that tournament became very popular. Later, in response to their poor play in the Mid-Winter, a group of gentlemen formed the Down and Out Club in 1907. Frank Presbrey continued to promote golf through tournament play, and his agency continued to be responsible for advertising and publicity until 1926.

On February 6, 1903, the first Inaugural Tournament was held at Pinehurst. An eighteen-hole medal play event with full handicaps, the Inaugural began the golf season and attracted players of national prominence such as Walter J. Travis, the 1900 and 1901 U.S. Amateur champion who would also win it for a third time later that year. By 1905 the tournament was renamed the Mid-Winter Championship. According to the *Pinehurst Outlook*, players were rated under the "Pinehurst system, meaning that the entries were classified according to their ability."

Walter J. Travis was one of the most influential golfers of the twentieth century. In addition to being an exceptional player and course designer, Travis was the founder and editor of *American Golfer* magazine and the author of two golf instruction books. He won the U.S. Amateur in 1900, 1901, and 1903. In 1904 he won the British Amateur and the Mid-Winter at Pinehurst.

At the same time that the Mid-Winter was becoming established, the North and South Open was starting up. It belonged to the Ross boys for a few years, with Donald being beaten by his brother Alex in 1902, Donald winning in 1903, Alex taking it again in 1904, Donald prevailing in 1905 and 1906, and Alex repeating in 1907 and 1908. In fact, the first nine Opens were won by Scottish pros.

The North and South tournaments, played on Pinehurst No. 2, grew to attract many great players—both in the amateur and professional events. Amateurs such as Travis, Chick Evans Jr., George Dunlap Jr. (winning his first at sixteen years of age), Harvie Ward, Bill Campbell, Billy Joe Patton, Jack Nicklaus, Curtis Strange, and Davis Love III were all North and South Amateur champions. Besides the Ross boys, Walter Hagen, Horton Smith, Byron Nelson, Sam Snead, and Ben Hogan won the North and South Open. Hogan's first victory as a professional, in fact, came at the 1940 event.

In November 1936 the PGA Championship was conducted on Pinehurst No. 2 with its new bermudagrass greens. Sixty-four players, including defending champion Johnny Revolta, teed it up at match play. Six days later, Denny Shute beat Jimmy

The first Women's North and South Amateur Championship was played in 1903. The clubhouse can be seen in the background.

Thomson 3 and 2 in the final match to claim the winner's share of the $9,200 purse.

In 1951 The Ryder Cup matches were held at Pinehurst on courses No. 1, No. 2, and No. 3. Prior to the event, the team from Great Britain and Ireland (GB&I) had arrived in New York on the Queen Mary. Both teams were wined and dined in New York City and Washington, D.C., and were received by President Harry Truman. Once in Pinehurst, the two teams were ensconced in the East Wing of the Carolina Hotel. With season tickets costing only $12.50, Richard Tufts (grandson of James) had to turn down requests for rooms because there weren't enough for all the people who wanted to attend the matches. There were so many spectators, in fact, that parking places were assigned at the Village Chapel, the tennis courts, and out toward the horse racing track. For those unable to attend, the event was covered by newspapers, the radio, and even television. Oddly, for the first and only time in Ryder Cup history, the matches were not conducted on consecutive days. Matches were played on November 2 and November 4 but not on November 3. That day the teams traveled to Chapel Hill to attend the Carolina-Tennessee football game. The Americans ended up winning the Ryder Cup by a score of $9^{1}/_{2}$ to $2^{1}/_{2}$.

Eleven years later, the U.S. Amateur Championship was conducted at Pinehurst No. 2. Again, for only $12.50, fans could attend every practice round and all six days of the tournament, plus receive a souvenir history of Pinehurst written by Richard Tufts. Twenty-year-old Labron Harris Jr. of Stillwater, Oklahoma—winner of the Oklahoma Amateur and medallist at the prestigious Western Amateur Championship—rounded out a good year by winning the U.S. Amateur with a 1-up victory in the final match over Downing Gray.

In 1994 the U.S. Senior Open was held on Pinehurst No. 2. South African Simon Hobday won by a shot over Jim Albus and Graham Marsh with a seventy-

Donald's brother Alex in 1907. Alex was a club professional for many years.

two-hole score of 274 (-14). Five years later (surprisingly, considering the course's long history and reputation), the U.S. Open was conducted on Pinehurst No. 2 for the very first time. Measuring much longer than it ever had in the past, and playing to a par of 70 (rather than its usual par of 72), No. 2 proved to be a stern test for the best golfers in the world. The happy winner, with a score of 279 (-1), was Payne Stewart—by a shot over Phil Mickelson. Sadly, only a couple of months later, the 1999 Open champion lost his life in a tragic airplane accident.

Today, a statue of Payne Stewart stands near the Pinehurst Country Club clubhouse.

The 1903 Women's North and South Amateur was won by New Jersey's Myra Patterson with a course record of 86. She successfully defended her title the following year and won it again in 1906.

The 1909 Women's North and South Amateur champion was Miss Mary Fownes of Oakmont, Pennsylvania

The North and South Open never failed to attract the top players. Walter Hagen won in 1918, 1921, and 1924 and was runner-up in 1920, 1925, and 1927.

After Charles "Chick" Evans won the North and South Amateur in 1911, one of his prizes was an airplane ride over Pinehurst with pilot Lincoln Beechy.

Glenna Collett Vare of Rhode Island won the North and South six times between 1922 and 1930.

Scotland's Dorothy Campbell Hurd won the Women's North and South Amateur in 1918, 1920, and 1921. Her favorite club was a mashie (5-iron) that she owned for over twenty years. She called it "Thomas."

During World War I, Scottish-born Tommy Armour lost the sight in one of his eyes. In spite of this, he managed to win three of golf's "majors" but never the North and South Open. His best finish at Pinehurst was runner-up in 1928 and 1929.

Armour and fellow Scot Bobby Cruickshank, winner of the North and South Open in 1926, 1927, and 1943.

George Dunlap Jr. was only sixteen when he became the youngest winner of the Mid-Winter tournament (he also won it three more times). In 1931 Dunlap (left) defeated Samuel Parks for his first victory in the North and South Amateur. He won again in 1933, 1934, 1935, 1936, 1940, and 1942.

Spectators watch the action during the 1931 Women's North and South Amateur Championship.

Henry Picard won the North and South Open in 1934 and 1936 and would eventually become a three-time major championship winner (1922 and 1939 PGA; 1938 Masters).

A gallery surrounds the fourteenth hole on the No. 3 course during the 1937 Women's North and South.

Glenna Collett Vare and Estelle Lawson Page, winner of the 1935, 1937, 1939, 1940, 1941, 1944, and 1945 Women's North and South Amateur tournaments.

Donald Ross (center) awarding
the medal for winning the
1937 North and South Open
to Horton Smith. Runner-up
Paul Runyan is at right

Frank Strafaci (left), 1939
Amateur winner, and runner-up
Bobby Dunkleberger.

Byron Nelson (right), 1939 North and South Open winner, and runner-up Horton Smith.

Ben Hogan's first victory as a professional came at the 1940 North and South Open. Donald Ross awarded the medal.

In 1903 participants practice for a putting contest prior to the inaugural Women's North and South Amateur Championship.

Hogan plays from a bunker during the 1940 North and South Open. He would win it again in 1942 and 1946.

Louise Suggs won the Women's North and South Amateur in 1942, 1946, and 1948. After she turned professional, she won eleven major championships.

Above: Maureen Orcutt, left, defeated Virginia Van Wie in the 1931 Women's North and South Amateur Championship. Miss Van Wie went on to win the U.S. Women's Amateur Championship three consecutive years (1932–1934) before retiring from competitive golf.

Peggy Kirk (left) won her only Women's North and South Amateur Championship in 1949. Estelle Lawson Page (right) won it seven times between 1939 and 1945.

Frank Stranahan came close to winning the Amateur in 1945, then won it in 1946, 1949, and 1952. A fitness buff, Stranahan kept in top shape. He's shown here lifting weights near the Carolina.

Toney Penna won the Open in 1948.

Babe and George Zaharias in 1947, following her victory in the Women's North and South Amateur at Pinehurst.

E. Harvie Ward, a member of the University of North Carolina golf team, came to Pinehurst to play in the 1948 North and South Amateur. With Chapel Hill just over an hour away, crowds of Ward's fellow students came to Pinehurst to watch him play and cheer him on.

Two years in a row (1948 and 1949), Frank Stranahan and Harvie Ward met in the finals of the North and South Amateur. Harvie defeated Frank in 1948; Frank beat Harvie in 1949.

Johnny Bulla, Sam Snead, Gene Sarazen, and Paul Runyan (left to right) wait to tee off in the 1949 North and South Open.

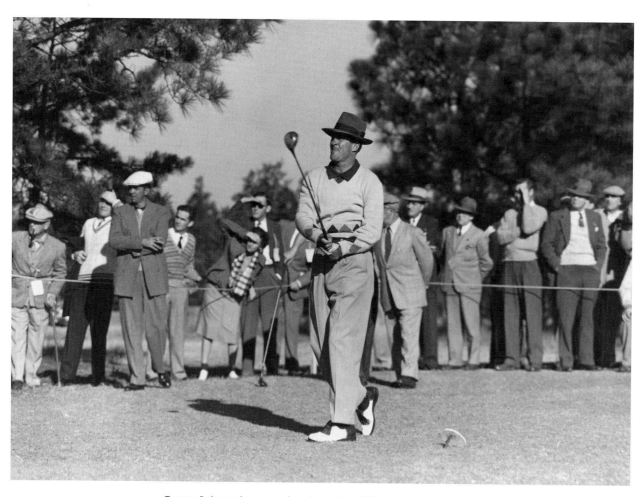

Tommy Bolt watches a tee shot during the 1951 North and South Open.

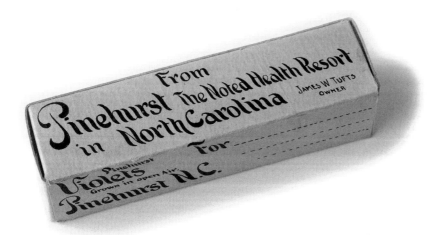

Barbara Romack, 1952 Amateur champion, and General George Marshall, Pinehurst resident and golf fan.

Left to right: John Barnum, runner-up; 1951 Open champ Tommy Bolt; Richard Tufts; low amateur "Bo" Winninger. It was the last time Tufts would award the first-place prize for the North and South Open. In 1952, the year of its fiftieth anniversary, the Open was replaced with the North and South Senior Championship.

Three-time major championship winner
Julius Boros was co-owner of Pine Needles
and Mid Pines and head pro at Mid Pines for
twenty years. In 1948 he was the runner-up
in the North and South Open.

Bill Campbell won the North and South Amateur in 1950, 1953, 1957, and 1967. Campbell (left) receives the Amateur trophy in 1953. The runner-up was Mal Galletta (right).

The leaderboard at the 1936 PGA Championship at Pinehurst No. 2.

Arnie and his dad, M. J. "Deke" Palmer.

Jack Nicklaus, 1959 North and South and U.S. Amateur champion. Jack's son, Jackie, won the North and South Amateur in 1985, making them the only father-and-son winners.

H. Dennsmore "Denny" Shute receives the Wanamaker Trophy for winning the 1936 PGA Championship at Pinehurst.

The Stars and Stripes and the Union Jack are raised in the opening ceremonies of the 1951 Ryder Cup at Pinehurst Country Club. During the matches, the No. 2 course played just over 7,000 yards.

The 1951 Ryder Cup team from Great Britain and Ireland: (Left to right) Harry Weetman, Max Faulkner, Jimmy Adams, John Panton, Fred Daly, Captain Arthur Lacey, Ken Bousfield, Dai Rees, Arthur Lees, Jack Hargreaves, and Charlie Ward.

The 1951 American Ryder Cup team: (Left to right) Jackie Burke, Ben Hogan, Ed "Porky" Oliver, Jimmy Demaret, Henry Ransom, Captain Sam Snead, Lloyd Mangrum, Clayton Heafner, Skip Alexander, and E.J. "Dutch" Harrison.

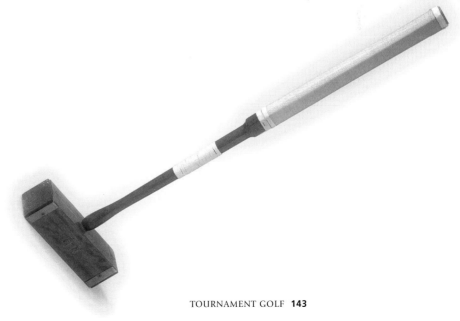

Walter Hagen and
Ben Hogan during the
Ryder Cup matches
in November.

Captain Sam Snead, Lloyd Mangrum, and friends watching
the Ryder Cup competition.

Presentation of the 1951 Ryder Cup. The galleries were larger than expected.

Sam Snead, the American captain, accepts the Ryder Cup trophy after the Americans defeated Great Britian and Ireland 9 1/2 to 2 1/2.

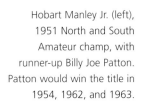

Hobart Manley Jr. (left), 1951 North and South Amateur champ, with runner-up Billy Joe Patton. Patton would win the title in 1954, 1962, and 1963.

Following his victory at the 1962 U.S. Amateur Championship at Pinehurst No. 2, Labron Harris Jr. is awarded the Havemeyer Trophy.

Mr. and Mrs. John Philip Sousa (the March King) and Mr. and Mrs. Leonard Tufts picnicking in Pinehurst.

Chapter 6

FAMOUS FACES

As a result of the quality and variety of activities available in the village and the continuous promotion of its attributes throughout the northern states, Pinehurst became a playground for the wealthy and the well-known. Golf was definitely the main attraction. The combination of Donald Ross' growing reputation as a master course designer, the number of good golf holes available, and the increasing popularity of the game made Pinehurst the place to be.

Captains of industry, politicians, sportsmen, entertainers, world leaders, and some of the best golfers in the world made Pinehurst their haunt. Famous and powerful people attracted even more famous and powerful people. Frank Presbrey, the advertising executive hired to publicize Pinehurst, knew that people liked to read about themselves and see their photos in newspapers and magazines. Every season, the *Pinehurst Outlook* printed the names of visitors to the village, how they got there, who they brought with them, how long they were staying, and which cottages they were staying in. Photos of these people with their guests—or with the people they had come to visit—were constantly in the newspaper. If some famous person had a dinner party, had guests arriving from far-off places, or was planning an exciting voyage, it was in the *Outlook*. Pinehurst photographer John Hemmer made a point of sending his photos to newspapers "up north" so that everyone back home could see what their friends and family were doing in Pinehurst. Dances, formals, and parties were conducted throughout the season, and "cottagers" made an occasion or a celebration out of almost everything.

Without a doubt, Pinehurst was the place to experience the good life.

James McCutcheon, the oldest representative of the Winter League of Advertisers, in his golf togs in January 1905.

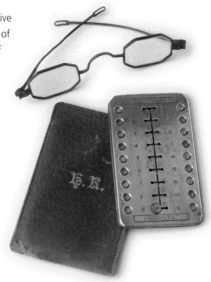

L. W. Maxwell, left, and Grantland Rice, foremost American sportswriter of his time.

Businessman Eberhard Faber takes time out for golf. Faber parlayed his great-grandfather's pencil business into a worldwide supplier of writing products and art supplies.

Donald Ross' brother
Alex won six North and
South Opens.

In 1913 Francis Ouimet stunned
the golf world when he won the
U.S. Open Championship as a
twenty-year-old amateur.

President Theodore Roosevelt visited Pinehurst twice: after leaving office in 1909 and before running again in 1912 on the Progressive (Bull Moose) ticket.

In 1916 Annie Oakley
and Frank Butler moved
to Pinehurst after leaving
Buffalo Bill's Wild West Show.
She began performing and
teaching at the Pinehurst
Gun Club. Two of her most
famous students were
John Philip Sousa and
John D. Rockefeller.

Annie Oakley and Frank
Butler were popular teachers
at the Gun Club. Annie
devoted much of her time to
teaching women to shoot.
They left Pinehurst in 1924,
both in failing health. Two
years later, they died within
weeks of each other.

At age fifteen, Annie Oakley challenged Frank Butler to a shooting match and won. He immediately became infatuated with her and they later married.

Actress Gloria Swanson came to Pinehurst in January 1926 to work on a motion picture. Some scenes were shot at McKenzie Mill in nearby Juniper Lake. She returned in March to perform at the Pinehurst Theater in a play called *The Untamed Lady*.

Blind and deaf since infancy, Helen Keller (right) became an author and an advocate for the visually impaired. She is shown here at the Carolina Hotel with, most likely, Polly Thomson, who traveled with Keller after Annie Sullivan became too ill.

Actor and social commentator Will Rogers (in chaps) came to Pinehurst in 1924 and 1925 to play polo. Both Leonard and Richard Tufts encouraged him to help publicize the sport at Pinehurst.

Will Rogers prepares to take a spin at the Pinehurst Flying Field with Lloyd Yost.

Amelia Earhart and her husband George Putnam were frequent guests at the Carolina. She flew her Beech-Nut Autogyro in and out of the Pinehurst Flying Field in the early 1930s. She is shown here with Lloyd Yost.

Walter Hagen tees off in the 1932 North and South Open. Hagen's swing was once described thus: "It begins with a sway and ends with a lunge."

Statesman Cordell Hull
refines his putting stroke
as Mrs. Hull looks on.

Donald Ross with Valerie
and Ben Hogan

Gene Tunney (left), world heavyweight boxing champion from 1926 to 1928, discusses his golf game with the Honorable Homer Cummings, U.S. Attorney General from 1934 to 1939.

Thomas Dewey, Republican presidential hopeful in 1944 and 1948, took time off from his prosecutorial duties to play golf at Pinehurst.

Five-star General Omar Bradley (center) visited Pinehurst during the 1953 North and South Senior Amateur Championship.

Richard Tufts (left), president of Pinehurst, Inc., and grandson of James Walker Tufts, waits to tee off.

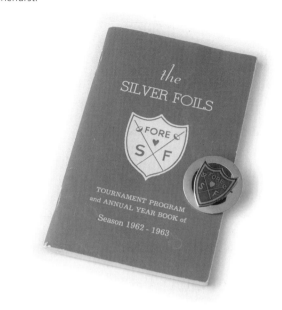

Bandleader Glenn Miller (right) also played golf at Pinehurst.

Walter Hagen, Bobby Cruickshank, Gene Sarazen, and Tommy Armour (left to right) visit during the 1951 Ryder Cup matches.

General and Mrs. George C. Marshall on the porch of their cottage, Liscombe Lodge, in Pinehurst.

Peggy and Warren "Bullet" Bell returning to Pinehurst. Peggy, of Pine Needles, was the first woman voted into the World Golf Teachers' Hall of Fame.

Bill Tilden, the first American to win at Wimbledon, competed frequently in Pinehurst. He was by far the best tennis player in the first half of the twentieth century.

Governor Channing Cox of Massachusetts, Donald Ross, Governor H. N. Spaulding of New Hampshire, and Governor Allan T. Fuller of Massachusetts (left to right). (Photo courtesy of the North Carolina Office of Archives and History.)

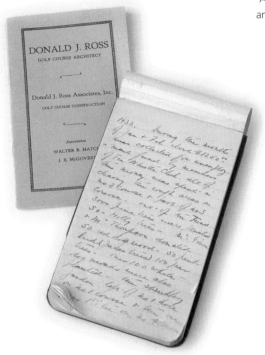

After the demise of the North and South Open, Richard Tufts concentrated on promoting senior and amateur golf.

Lou Worsham, Clayton Heafner, George Fazio, and Jackie Burke (left to right) enjoy a round of golf at Pinehurst.

Presidential candidate Adlai Stevenson takes a break from politics at Pinehurst.

Actors Ann Jeffries and Robert Sterling, stars of the television show *Topper*, enjoyed golf at Pinehurst.

Radio and television star Edgar Bergen, with sidekick "Charlie McCarthy" at Pinehurst.

Judy Bell (left), future first woman president of the USGA, and Barb McIntire, 1959 and 1964 winner of the U.S. Women's Amateur Championship.

North Carolina Senator Sam Ervin (second from left) and Senator Joseph O. Mahoney of Wyoming (second from right) meet with local business owners at the Carolina Hotel.

Queen Frederica of the Hellenes, queen of Greece, with Mrs. George C. Marshall at the Marshalls' home in Pinehurst.

Avid golfer President Dwight D. Eisenhower visiting Pinehurst.

Ben Hogan enjoys some
Southern hospitality during
the 1951 Ryder Cup.

Gene Sarazen and Sam Snead
warming up on Maniac Hill.

Movie actor Don Ameche (right) enjoyed golf with friends at Pinehurst.

Reverend Billy Graham (second from left) was the first Western Christian leader to speak in public behind the Iron Curtain. Here, the evangelist spreads the word about Pinehurst.

Margaret Truman Daniels, daughter of President Harry S. Truman, visiting the Carolina Hotel. Mrs. Daniels is the author of many mystery novels and several political books.

Vice President Richard M. Nixon also enjoyed a few rounds on Pinehurst No. 2.

Peter Tufts (left), great-grandson of James Walker Tufts, discusses the Putter Boy with Mr. and Mrs. Chic Young. Young was the creator of the comic strip "Blondie."

Fifteen-time All Star catcher Yogi Berra putting at Pinehurst.

The Sandhill Fair was first held in 1914 and was sponsored by the Sandhills Board of Trade and the Sandhills Farmers' Association. Originally the fair was a pageant to celebrate the history of North Carolina. A contest was also held to determine the most comely lady in the Sandhills to represent the fair.

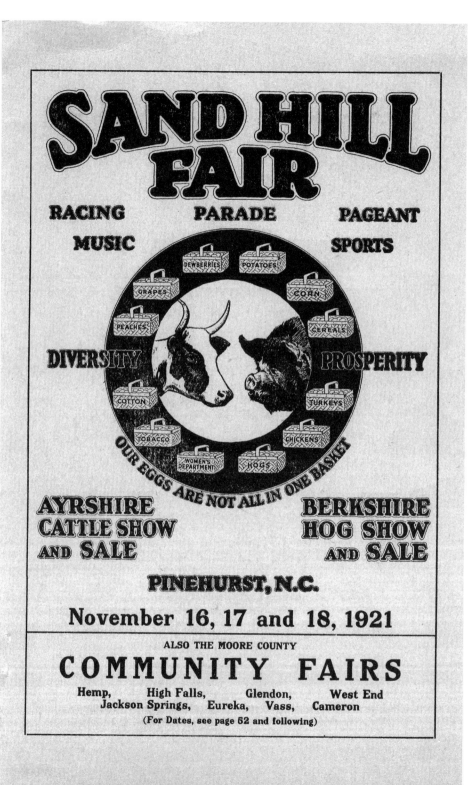

Chapter 7
LEISURE TIME

When James Walker Tufts purchased the land for his village, he had long dreamed of creating a health spa for consumptives. He hoped to build a New England–style town in a southern climate. Almost before the paint was dry, it was learned that consumption (tuberculosis) was contagious. Tufts was suddenly faced with the problem of what to do to make people want to come to his village, and to want to stay.

Just before the turn of the twentieth century, the concept of leisure time was almost unknown to the general population. Many northeasterners, however, were in the habit of going south to escape the New England winters. Tufts had to make them want to stop halfway to Florida, and make them like it. He knew he had to provide distraction and entertainment for the guests. He wanted people to think of coming to Pinehurst for recreational purposes, and he started with golf.

In an effort to promote the game, a variety of tournaments was offered. The village advertised heavily in northern publications. As the fields of golfers grew, so did the quality of play, and better golfers were attracted in greater numbers. The highest-caliber players came to Pinehurst. The newspaper was filled with photos of the tournament winners and photos of the trophies to be awarded each season.

At the same time, Tufts began to promote other sports and leisure activities. Wildlife was abundant and hunting and shooting became popular. A racetrack was also built, and harness racing, flat racing, and horse training grew until the best horses in the sport were coming to Pinehurst to train. Gymkhana was the term for a number of contests involving stunts performed with horses, pigs, mules, wheelbarrows, and just about anything else anyone could think of. Gymkhanas were held regularly at Pinehurst. Fox hunting was also widespread. The Archers Company was persuaded to open a business on Midland Road in Pinehurst, and archery lessons and tournaments became quite popular. Some visitors even played archery golf.

The Sandhill Fair became a showplace for horticulture, agriculture, and animal husbandry. The fair began with a parade that included local beauties.

In addition, a performance ring was built at the Carolina Hotel, and dog shows, horse shows, and pet shows were regular events. The Sandhill Fair was also started during Pinehurst's early days and grew to be one of the finest of its time, attended by thousands of people. Tennis courts were built, and the best tennis players began coming to Pinehurst to play. Not surprisingly, the first miniature golf course in America was built in Pinehurst.

A theater was also built in Pinehurst so that residents and guests could enjoy live performances and the latest motion pictures. There were also tournaments for bridge, ping-pong, and bingo. Any event, in fact—from the birth of the smallest peep at the poultry farm to a total eclipse of the sun—was the opportunity for a celebration. Leisure became an art in Pinehurst.

A crowd of over 3,000 attended the first Sandhill Fair. Chauffeurs drove as many as nine carloads from Southern Pines, and attendees ranged from "the common hardworking farmer" to "prominent men of the communities." In 1922 a man whom Leonard Tufts invited to the fair replied, "Nothing can keep us away because we want to see your beautiful fair…and want to see your progressive young city, Pinehurst."

In 1915 it must have been quite a thrill to see a camel in the Carolina Desert.

Pinehurst, NC
Fox

A trained bear was another exciting attraction. The motto of the fair had become "Bigger, Better and More Interesting Than Ever." Before long, however, the Sandhill Fair began to cost more than it brought in.

Because the Tufts family believed strongly in the benefits of recreation, athletic events were always a part of life in the village. The area attracted horsemen and women from near and far. The show ring at the Carolina, the playing fields, and the horse track were always busy. Guests and participants could also enjoy a spirited mule race at the track.

Sometimes a good deal of pigsmanship was required as well.

Most of the stunts required skilled horsemanship and agility.

In the 1920s Leonard and Richard Tufts began promoting polo at Pinehurst. As the sport became more popular, polo clubs from throughout the south came to Pinehurst to play matches. James Walker Tufts' grandson, James, was very involved in polo matches until the early 1940s. During World War II, only exhibition matches were held.

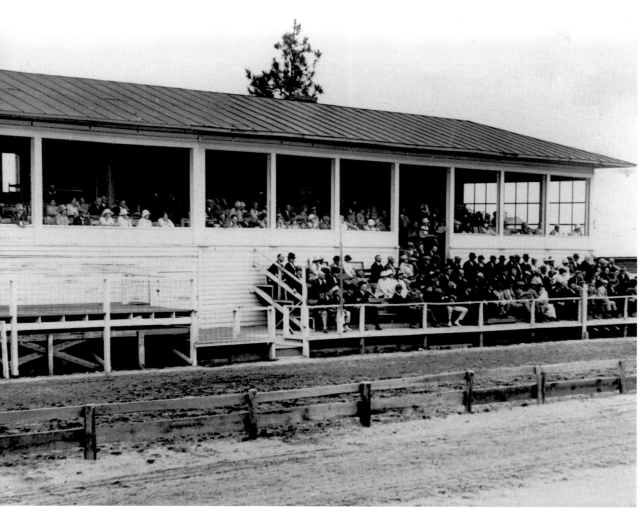

There were two racetracks built in 1916. The inside track was a half-mile long and was for trotters and pacers. The outer track was five-eighths of a mile long and was for thoroughbreds. Some of the greatest horses in the sport were trained in Pinehurst. The soft, sandy terrain was favored by trainers for breaking in yearlings and for the development of healthy musculature.

The mild climate and facilities made the Pinehurst track a favorite. In 1952 the Pinehurst Driving and Training Club began a lease of the track that lasted forty years. By the end of the 1950s, about 300 horses were stabled and in training at the track. In 1988 the Friends of the Track began to pressure the village to purchase the facility, which also had become a habitat for the endangered red-cockaded woodpecker. After the purchase was made a few years later, the Pinehurst Racetrack was placed on the National Register of Historic Places.

Non-participants came out in their finery to enjoy the races.

All manner of spectators
enjoyed an afternoon
at the races.

A show ring was
located at the Carolina
Hotel as well.

The ring was used for a variety of activities, including equestrian events.

Most holidays and other special occasions featured a Pet Show at the Carolina for locals and guests.

A dog show at the Fair Barn. During the Sandhill Fair, the barn was used to display rows of canned and preserved goods. Leonard Tufts was instrumental in attracting many conventions and meetings on agriculture and the care and breeding of hogs and cattle to the village.

The dog and horse shows were serious business, but occasionally there was some monkeying around.

Bud Wicker boarded and trained dogs for Leonard Tufts. The dogs competed in events put on by the Pinehurst Field Trial Club and other clubs. Due to the dogs' frequent and annoying barking, however, some guests and residents questioned Wicker's training skills.

Fox hunting was and still is very popular in the Sandhills. The actual hunt was only a portion of the festivities, however. Breakfasts, formal balls, and other social events were also part of the hunt.

Once they picked up the scent, no barrier was too tough for the hounds.

Wild turkey and other game were abundant around Pinehurst, and hunting was a popular pastime.

The Pinehurst Gun Club was founded in 1898 and formally organized in 1904. Leonard Tufts was the first president. Guests that weren't interested in golf or other activities could shoot at clay targets.

Mr. and Mrs. Frank Butler (Annie Oakley) arrived in Pinehurst in 1916. Annie managed the trap and rifle range, and Frank handled the skeet facility.

Annie taught women to shoot because she believed they should be able to defend themselves. In 1921 she was injured in a car accident and never fully recovered. Eventually, she returned home to Ohio and died there in 1926.

Philip Rounsevelle, the operator of the Archers Company in Pinehurst, kept over 300 varieties of wood on hand from as far off as Scotland and Surinam. He claimed that a good bow could shoot an arrow up to 460 yards.

The first Mid-Winter Archery Tournament was held at Pinehurst in 1927. General Ivor Thord Gray set a world record and helped create interest in the sport.

As the sport gained in popularity, women wanted to participate as well. Even Glenna Collett Vare (second from left) took time out from golf to practice her archery.

In 1932 a nine-hole Archery Golf tournament was added. The players shot arrows instead of hitting golf balls and a target was placed over the hole.

Tennis was another popular sport in Pinehurst. The original tennis courts were below the clubhouse and tournaments were held frequently.

A tennis tournament in 1936 drew a large gallery.

Lawn bowling was another way to spend a beautiful afternoon in Pinehurst.

During the season, Pinehurst's social calendar was always full, with frequent dress balls and formal parties held at the Carolina Hotel.

Even the children participated in the social events and galas.

Theme parties like this barn dance were always welcome and well attended.

There were numerous opportunities to dress in costume as well, with parties for youngsters and even employees.

Costume parties were very popular, and participants put great effort into the perfect costume. This woman sports the Tin Whistles logo on her golf bag costume.

This woman wears the perfect costume for an event in Pinehurst.

Many of the costumes reflected current events, like this Charlie McCarthy/Edgar Bergen duo.

Mr. and Mrs. James Tufts enjoy one of the many hat parties held at the Carolina.

The Carolina Hotel hosted many entertaining activities for guests and employees. This revue featured exotic dancers.

Here guests vie for championship status at the ping-pong table.

Bingo was a weekly attraction. Talented players became regulars and often worked on several cards at the same time.

Bridge tournaments at the Carolina were always well attended.

Carriage rides and hayrides have always been a part of leisure activities in the village.

The designated driver was already in vogue in Pinehurst in the early 1950s.

JOHN G. HEMME
PINEHURST, N.C.

Miniature golf got its start at Pinehurst in 1916, when James Barber, president of Barber Steamship Lines, decided to build a small golf course in the back of his village estate. The story goes that he hired an architect, Edward H. Wiswell, to lay out the course. When it was completed, Barber supposedly looked it over and announced, "This'll do." The course, the first of its kind in America, immediately was named Thistle Dhu, and was the site of many unique parties and tournaments.

Hooray, hooray, it's the first of May! Children circle the Maypole on the Village Green.

Race fans have a side wager during lulls in the schedule.

Cottagers could pass a pleasant afternoon at Watson's Lake.

In 1900 there was a total eclipse of the sun visible in Pinehurst. The Naval Observatory outfitted an expedition with two 6-inch Dallmeyer lenses, a 4-inch Voigtlaender lens, and a 40-foot photo-heliograph. The heliograph was mounted atop a tower that was specially built to view the eclipse. The outside of the tower supported the tube of the camera, and the inside held the lens.

The Pinehurst expedition was assigned the duty of drawing the corona, using the naked eye as well as the telescopic lens.

After an afternoon at the races or a long trail ride, a rest in the shade was perfect.

ACKNOWLEDGMENTS

A work of this nature takes an effort by many. First and foremost, I would like to thank Mildred McIntosh, secretary to Richard S. Tufts, for saving the records, documents, and images that are housed in the Tufts Archives. She is personally responsible for retrieving them from a garbage dump where they had been sent by the new Pinehurst regime in the early 1970s. Without the wonderful images taken by a handful of creative photographers over the years, this book could not exist. It would have been tragic to lose those priceless materials.

I wish to acknowledge the excellent work of the people that have preceded me; I have benefited from their diligence. Thanks also to our wonderful volunteers, who work like slaves and love it.

The person who initiated this project was Tom Stewart, Pinehurst resident, businessman, and Archives board member. Tom knew there was a book here and that it was an opportunity to raise money for the Archives.

I also want to thank the late Fred Haenlein, who did research for the Tufts Archives for more than seven years. Liz Dowling, John Root, Ernie Lorenzen, Gary Edquist, and Sue Loth helped answer my questions. Barb Newton scanned documents until her eyes crossed, Larry Watson stayed up late to scan smudged and stained images, and my husband, Jim, helped me wade through the many, many unidentified photos of the Pinehurst courses.

Thank you all. I am grateful for your help.